BRITAIN'S HERITAGE

The Tommy of the First World War

Neil R. Storey

AMBERLEY

Above: A French-produced greetings postcard for Tommies to send home from the trenches, 1915.

All images are from the author's own archive unless annotated otherwise.

First published 2017

Amberley Publishing
The Hill, Stroud
Gloucestershire, GL5 4EP

www.amberley-books.com

ISBN 978 1 4456 6987 8 (paperback)
ISBN 978 1 4456 6988 5 (ebook)

British Library Cataloguing in Publication Data.
A catalogue record for this book is available from the British Library.

Printed in the UK.

Contents

1

Introduction: Tommy Atkins and the British Army

This book is a brief overview of the story of the recruitment, equipment, training and experiences soldiers of the British line infantry regiments in the First World War. I fully acknowledge corps such as the Royal Artillery, Royal Engineers, Royal Army Medical Corps and Army Service Corps did sterling work – they undoubtedly knew the front lines and all their dangers too; indeed, their role in the Great War deserves a volume in their own right – but this book focuses on the front-line fighting Tommies, of what the corps men often referred to as 'the poor bloody infantry'.

The sobriquet 'Tommy Atkins' appears to have been applied to the soldiers of the British Army since the eighteenth century, but exactly how the name became adopted remains shrouded in military myth and legend. One story is that it came from the Duke of Wellington himself, who as a young officer was struck by the fortitude and stoicism of the men under his command, qualities epitomised in a man he found lying mortally wounded in the mud after the Battle of Boxtel in 1794. Seeing the concern on Wellington's face the soldier assured him, 'It's all right, sir, all in a day's work.' Years later, when the Duke was asked to suggest a name to be used in the book to show soldiers how their pocket book and other military forms should be filled out he remembered that dying soldier in the mud from all those years before – a certain Thomas Atkins. At least, that is according to one version of the story. In reality, there are examples of the term 'Tommy Atkins' being applied to British soldiers from the 1740s. Wherever it came from the name has stuck, for better or for worse.

In the nineteenth century the British Army enacted a number of reforms that not only saw improvements in weaponry, equipment

'The Veteran's Farewell: Good Bye, my lad. I only wish I were young enough to go with you!' and similar images showing veterans of past wars proudly wishing departing soldiers well were popular illustrations on recruiting posters and in magazines in 1914. (Library of Congress)

'History and Traditions' and the rarer 'Soldier's Pay' postcards produced by Gale & Polden in the early twentieth century provide fine colour images of the army of the day in their dress uniforms.

and uniform, but also introduced education, physical development and fitness for soldiers, temperance, provision of better food, good Christian values, clear regulations and a more regulated day-to-day routine encompassing a variety of skills including drill, training, P.T., route marches, duties and maintenance of personal kit and equipment that kept soldiers occupied and instilled discipline worthy of the greatest army in the world.

Campaigns and 'small wars', notably in India and Africa, were also fought by the Army, to acquire, protect and maintain British rule over its Empire. Reigning majestically over it all was Her Majesty Queen Victoria. British Tommies, with their distinctive scarlet tunics, were every bit 'Soldiers of the Queen' and their grand parades at state occasions and Durbars truly made the 'spectacle of Empire' something remarkable to behold. But the grand show of scarlet tunics synonymous with the British Army the world over was rapidly disappearing from the battlefield as warfare changed from huge set piece battles and forming square to more fluid engagements and attacks while on campaign across Africa and India.

Khaki (a corruption of an Urdu or Hindi word meaning dust coloured) uniforms had been worn by some regiments from as early as the Indian Mutiny in 1858 but were formally introduced for wear by British units in India in 1878 and scarlet jackets were retained predominantly for troops on home service and parades.

The greatest reforms to the British Army during the nineteenth century were introduced by Secretary of State for War Edward Cardwell between 1868 and 1874. Under Cardwell's localisation scheme, the country was divided into sixty-six Brigade Districts (later renamed Regimental Districts), based on county boundaries and population density. All line infantry regiments would now consist of two battalions sharing a depot and associated recruiting area.

Officers and Men of 2nd Battalion, The Norfolk Regiment, at their foreign service depot, Belgaum, India, 1912. (Library of Congress)

One battalion would serve overseas, while the other was stationed at home for training. The Militia of the area usually became the third battalion. Cardwell's reforms were continued by Secretary of State for War Hugh Childers, who abolished regimental seniority numbers in 1881, and forthwith regiments were to be known by their regimental district names instead – e.g. The East Surrey Regiment, The Lincolnshire Regiment or The Dorset Regiment.

Despite some improvements in sobriety and education both in and outside the army, the South African War (1899–1902) exposed weaknesses and inefficiency in the ranks due to poor literacy, numeracy and the health of its volunteers. The Esher Report collated what was learned and made a number of recommendations, most notably a brand-new approach to the organisation, recruit selection process, training and organisation of the British Army. Richard Burdon Haldane, the new Liberal Government's Secretary of War, had the duty of implementing these recommendations.

Haldane began by creating an Officer Training Corps (OTC) in 1907 with a view to creating a 'seed bed' of young officers for the reformed army. The movement had two divisions: 'Senior', based in Universities, and 'Junior', working in public and grammar schools. Every week the boys would parade for drill and marching, learn skill at arms, have shooting practice at their local range and would regularly go off on manoeuvres across the school field and nearby heath land. There would also be spring and summer OTC camps with other schools. Haldane's vision matured in 1914 and in the first seven months of the war, the OTC provided over 20,000 commissioned officers. Many of them joined their regiments straight from school and school 'Old Boys' clubs circulated appeals to their members to 'rally to the flag.'

The greatest task implemented by Haldane was to be the complete reorganisation of the Home Field Army and Reserve System. Under the new scheme all regiments would have

Recruiting poster for the Regular Army, 1914.

two Regular Army battalions, one of which would provide garrison troops for the Empire while the other battalion would become part of a standing 'Home Service' army in Britain and Ireland that would, in the event of a 'war emergency,' form a British Expeditionary Force ready for deployment to anywhere on the continent. Every line infantry soldier in the Regular Army would have volunteered, and 'signed on the dotted line' for, at least the minimum term of seven years 'with the colours' with five on the Reserve.

Those who had left the army but were retained on the Reserve could be called up to bring the Regular Army up to full strength. Reservists were classified into four categories: 'A' – those who could be immediately called for any minor emergency, 'B' – the general reserve, 'C' – general service men transferred prematurely, and 'D' – men whose time on the Reserve had expired but volunteered to remain on call for another four years. Alongside them were the Special Reserve, previously known as 'militia men', who had volunteered to keep their names on the Reserve.

The new Territorial Force, in the event of a war emergency, would be mobilised to become a full-time army capable of taking the place of the regular battalions to defend Britain. The Territorial Force was not intended to serve abroad. In 1907 there were 221 battalions of volunteer infantry in England, Scotland and Wales. The reformed line infantry regiments' battalions were given sequential numbers – e.g. 1st and 2nd Battalions were the Regulars, the 3rd became a Reserve Battalion and the Territorials 4th and 5th Battalions. New units that consisted of all Territorial Force soldiers were also created, namely the Monmouthshire, Cambridgeshire, Hertfordshire and Herefordshire Regiments and the many battalions of the London Regiment. There were also eleven much-heralded Territorial Force Cyclist battalions allocated to county regiments across Britain.

Haldane backed up his reforms by standardising training and procedure in the Army by creating, with his team of military advisers, a raft of official manuals laying down in detail everything from drill, skill at arms and musketry, to staff responsibilities and procedures. Armed with these volumes, no-one could be left under any illusions of how the men were to be trained, how the chain of command worked, how soldiers should be managed in the field, and how warfare should be conducted.

Above: Territorial Force soldiers of 5th Battalion, Loyal North Lancashire Regiment (T.F.), at training camp at Hornby, 1919.
Below: Signallers and scouts of 6th Battalion, Northumberland Fusiliers (T.F.), with their bicycles, 1910.

Coldstream Guards marching out wearing 'manoeuvre bands' in their hats during the Great Manoeuvres of September 1912 – the last major British Army exercise before the outbreak of the First World War.

Prospective recruits for the Territorial Force had to be aged between seventeen and thirty-five, with a minimum chest measurement of thirty-three inches, a minimum height of five feet two inches, and would be required to enlist for a minimum of four years. Upon joining, the recruit was obliged to attend forty drills in his first year of enlistment. The weekly 'Drill nights' would usually be held at a local purpose-built drill hall or suitable public building such as a Corn Hall where he would learn parade-ground manoeuvres, discipline and marching. Recruits would also receive instruction and be required to pass the course of musketry held on two appointed afternoons through the summer months. The regular weekend manoeuvres undertaken by the soldiers of the Territorial Force earned them the nickname of 'Saturday Night Soldiers'.

Uniform was standard for the English and Welsh Territorials who were issued with the same khaki serge 'service dress' uniform jacket, trousers, stiff peaked cap and puttees as the regular soldiers, but many units asked their Territorial soldiers to provide their own shirts and boots. Along with the basic uniform they also had a greatcoat, waterproof cape and a set of 1908 pattern webbing. Their best parade and 'walking out' dress consisted of a blue, stiff peaked cap, red frock tunic with regimental coloured facings at collar and cuffs, trousers with a narrow red stripe at the sides, boots, buttons, and badges. In the case of Scottish regiments, the trousers were mostly replaced with kilts, socks, puttees and spats. Tunics frequently had the 'cut away' to the front flaps of the jacket and a variety of glengarries and Tam o' Shanters were worn as per regimental distinctions, traditions and standing orders.

A private soldier would draw a shilling a day, Corporals 1*s* 8*d*, Sergeants 2*s* 4*d*, up to Colour Sergeants on 3*s* 6*d* plus an additional three shillings for those who attended camp for 'wear and tear of boots.' The members of the cyclist battalions did especially well; each man had to own his own bicycle and his allowance for use of his bike at camp was the grand sum of £1 for eight days and 1*s* 6*d* for each subsequent day.

Above: Bedfordshire Regiment Territorial Force Battalion Machine Gun Section *c.* 1910. Pre-war machine guns were not easy to transport and took more than one man to operate them efficiently.
Left: A father and son in the Drums of a Territorial Force Battalion of the Northumberland Fusiliers *c.* 1913. Territorial Battalions were made up of friends, neighbours and extended family members from the local communities where they were based.

Above: Officers (seated front row centre) and sergeants of the Cambridgeshire Regiment (T.F.) in their dress uniforms *c.* 1914.
Right: Colour Party and Escorts, 1st Battalion, the Hertfordshire Regiment (T.F), *c.* 1910.

The summer of 1914 was beautifully sunny and Territorials would reflect on the summer camps of 1914 as some of the very best they had ever known, but they would also recall how it had been marred by the spectre of war hanging over it. Dislike and mistrust of Germans had been rumbling around for years in newspaper reportage, magazine stories and novels, but after the assassination of Archduke Franz Ferdinand, heir to the Austro-Hungarian throne, on 28 June 1914 it was soon apparent that it was no longer a matter of if there would be war, but when.

Above: The East Anglian Territorial Force Brigade march past the Earl of Leicester and General Inglefield at Holkham, July 1914.
Left: The message was clear – 'Your King and Country Need You' recruiting poster, November 1914.

2
Mobilisation

Over the month of July 1914, the permanent staff of the Territorial Infantry Brigades set up offices in many key towns, often immediately after their summer camps had ended. The adjutants of Territorial Force Battalions made arrangements to place themselves in close contact with their respective headquarters near post offices who would extend the hours of their telegraph service in the event of urgent announcements or orders being transmitted.

A 'Precautionary Period' was declared for Regular Army units on 27 July 1914. Mobilisation had not been ordered but it gave a fair warning to get everything in hand to make this as smooth as possible. On 30 July, Special Duty Companies of the Territorial Force were deployed to a number of places around the British coast to reassure the public and keep a weather eye out to sea, watching for invasion craft or spy activity. Most of the soldiers involved were left wondering what they could do in their tiny numbers if an invasion had come but they enjoyed the attention paid to them by the public as they took up their positions on guard duty.

Over the weekend of 1/2 August, a palpable military presence was felt in both coastal and urban areas as soldiers were posted to guard railway stations, utilities, wireless stations and military installations. On Monday 3 August 1914, Germany had requested that Belgium let its troops pass through, but Belgium had categorically refused and asked Britain to intervene to request an assurance that Belgian wishes would be respected. The request was sent and the world watched and waited for the response.

During the day of 4 August 1914, cities and towns were set abuzz as posters went up announcing the mobilisation of the Army Reserve and many a street resounded with knocks at the door from police officers delivering call-up notices to Reservists. The *Newcastle Journal* captured the moment:

> There was no mistaking these Reservists, for all their civilian attire. They had the upright carriage and swinging step that proclaimed the old soldier at once. Some of them were accompanied by their wives, many of them with young children clinging to their skirts, there was many a moving scene as the women dashed the tears from their eyes as they bade their 'bonny lad' go and do his duty.

At 11.00 p.m. on 4 August 1914 a state of war was declared with Germany and the Territorial Force was given the order: 'Mobilise.' The Territorial Force had, as part of its Regulations, clear directions and forms to use for mobilisation. Adjutants for every Territorial Force battalion already had the call-up notices stating where the men should report – all that would be required was the time to be written on it, a date stamp and a signature. Addressed envelopes, kept in the same order as the nominal rolls, had also been prepared and the appointed NCOs and men of the battalion worked into the early hours of the morning to get them out to every man of the battalion so they would be ready to report in the morning. Officers of the battalion were notified by telegram.

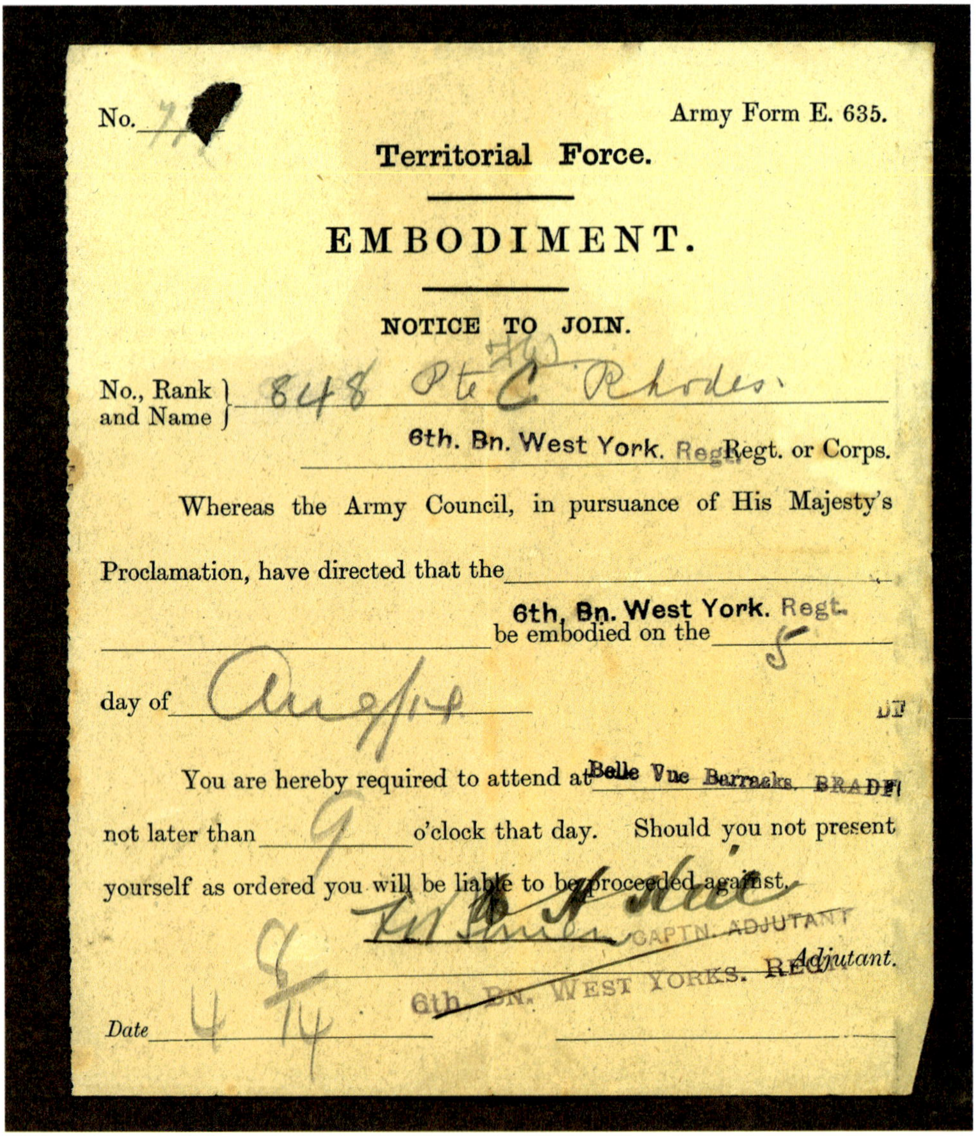

No.

Army Form E. 635.

Territorial Force.

EMBODIMENT.

NOTICE TO JOIN.

No., Rank and Name } 848 Pte C Rhodes

6th. Bn. West York. Reg. Regt. or Corps.

Whereas the Army Council, in pursuance of His Majesty's Proclamation, have directed that the 6th. Bn. West York. Regt. be embodied on the 5 day of August

You are hereby required to attend at Belle Vue Barracks. BRADF[illegible] not later than 9 o'clock that day. Should you not present yourself as ordered you will be liable to be proceeded against.

CAPTN. ADJUTANT 6th BN. WEST YORKS. REGT.

Adjutant.

Date 4/8/14

One of thousands of notices sent out to the men of the Territorial Force on the night of 4 August 1914 ordering their mobilisation. This example was sent to Pte. Cecil Rhodes, 6th Battalion, West Yorkshire Regiment (T.F.).

Every Territorial soldier had already been issued with a mobilisation checklist. Locally printed on card or paper for each unit, it clearly stated what uniform he would be expected to wear as well as the kit he should be carrying when reporting for duty on mobilisation. A typical list appeared on the back of the mobilisation notices for 6th Battalion, Northumberland Fusiliers:

> Dress:- Service dress and cap, Puttees, Waistbelt, Frog, Pouches, Bandolier, Haversack, Mess Tin, Waterbottle (filled), Great Coat (in carrier), Straps and Slings, Boots.

Equipment:- 1 Flannel Shirt, 1 pair Socks, 2 Towels, 1 Comb, 1 Razor, 1 Shaving Brush, 1 Tooth Brush, 1 Housewife [sewing kit] , 1 pair Boot Laces, 1 Table Knife, 1 Fork, 1 Spoon, 1 Holdall, 1 Clasp Knife.

If you have a pair of field glasses, compass or a cyclists' road map of the district, bring them with you.

All NCOs should bring a Note Book and Pencil.

Put some food in your Haversack.

The morning of 5 August 1914 saw many town and city marketplaces crowded with well-wishers watching the soldiers muster on parade. Often a local dignitary would give a short speech and the rector blessed the men before they marched off to the railway station to travel to their battalion headquarters.

Once there they would be put through a medical examination to check basic fitness for duty and to make sure the recruit had no contagious diseases or bodily infestations. Examination passed, the soldier would be issued with an identity disc and soldier's pay book, a rifle, and 100 rounds of ammunition. The soldiers would then march off in companies or battalions to their billets. These would vary greatly from place to place; the drill halls could not accommodate the numbers of men involved so schools, some public buildings, warehouses and maltings were the sort of buildings requisitioned for the purpose.

The War Office knew that Territorial soldiers were under no obligation to fight overseas but, knowing the 'call may come', a general appeal was put out to the Territorial battalions for volunteers for overseas service. The response was very positive, with many Territorial battalions sending in returns of around 90 per cent volunteering to 'do their bit overseas.'

Mobilised Norfolk Regiment Reservists departing to join the 1st Battalion for active service as part of the British Expeditionary Force, Thorpe Station, Norwich, August 1914.

Above: The people of King's Lynn throng the station to give their departing local Territorial Force companies a rousing farewell, 5 August 1914.
Left: Thousands of men bade farewell to their loved ones as they proceeded to war service and numerous postcards with sentimental verses were produced for them to send home.

Above left: Bamforth Song Cards (usually sold in sets of three, one for each verse) printed the popular songs of the day on postcards, illustrated to reflect the songs and the sentiment of the time.
Above right: A sergeant from a Lincolnshire Regiment Territorial Force battalion proudly wearing his 'Imperial Service' badge above his right breast pocket.
Below: The 'Imperial Service' badge presented to soldiers of the Territorial Force who volunteered to serve overseas.

Private, 2nd/7th (Cyclist) Battalion, the Welsh Regiment (T.F.), on coastal defence duty, 1916.

A white, metal pin-backed badge bearing the legend 'Imperial Service' surmounted by a crown was issued to those who so volunteered before 30 September 1914, and was worn with great pride above the right pocket on the tunic.

Very few Territorial units were to see action in the opening battles of the First World War; instead they were tasked with the duties for which they were originally raised – guarding the homeland. Most Territorial Force Battalions would leave their headquarters towns for 'war stations' over the next seven to ten days. Some were deployed to coastal defence duties; others dug trenches and provided a military presence inland.

The dislocation of men from their local environment also encouraged them to work as a unit away from the distractions of being close to home. Many of the Territorial cyclist battalions were deployed in patrolling the coast to provide the 'first line' in the event of an invasion.

From 1915, however, as the war widened, many Territorial Battalions were deployed to France and Flanders and provided major quotas for the campaigns in Gallipoli (1915) and Palestine (1917–18).

The tremendous expansion of the Territorial Force (T.F.) is often overshadowed by the recruiting campaign to raise Kitchener's New Armies but it should not be forgotten that by the end of September 1914 most T.F. Battalions had not only filled their existing battalion quotas but had also raised at least one reserve battalion for each. To avoid confusion the T.F. battalions were given numbers – e.g. 1/4th Battalion was the original first line Territorial unit that could be deployed abroad. The 2/4th and even 3/4th Battalions were the Reserve Battalions, raised with the intention of training recruits, ready to supply the first line battalion with reinforcements when required.

Did you know?

During times of high intakes and depleted stores during the early years of the First World War up to twenty-two men were known to have shared a single bell tent during training.

Above: Mud on their boots before the front line – soldiers from an Essex Regiment Territorial Force battalion during training in the UK, 1915.
Below left: Sergeant Instructors: Bombing, left and Musketry right, 2/7th Battalion, the Manchester Regiment (T.F.), 1915.
Below right:A typical sentimental card sent by soldiers in tented camps to loved ones back home (1914).

Above left: Some of the lads of 6th Battalion, West Yorkshire Regiment (T.F.), Strensall Camp, 1914.
Above right: Kitchener recruiting postcard, 1914.

In practice, however, some of these battalions did proceed abroad in their own right or once the men were trained cadres of the A1 soldiers were sent to serve with other active service battalions of the parent regiment and could well be called upon to supply men for others. This also happened to men in Kitchener's Army and to conscripts and is why many of our First World War ancestors may well have first joined their local regiment and trained with them. Their first photographs in uniform will show the local cap badge, but when the call for active service came they were drafted to a completely different regiment.

This did not always go down well with the men and later recruiting campaigns for the New Armies picked up on this, placing emphasis on the message in their recruiting posters and adverts – 'Those who join together serve together.'

3
Kitchener's Army

On 5 August 1914, the day after the announcement of the outbreak of the First World War, Field Marshal Earl Kitchener of Khartoum was formally appointed Secretary of State for War. For the people of Britain, it appeared a wise choice. Kitchener, or 'K of K' (Kitchener of Khartoum) as he was often known, was an established national hero who had come to prominence during the colonial small wars of the latter half of the nineteenth century, notably at the legendary Battle of Omdurman. He was every inch the epitome of the senior British Army officer, his face regularly featured in newspapers, magazines and on all manner of patriotic souvenirs from school reward certificates and decorative plates to matchbox holders, ceramic figurines and tea caddies. Kitchener was one of the few senior officers to be far sighted enough to see the war was certainly not going to be over by Christmas and that to have sufficient numbers of trained soldiers to fight for Britain he would have to step up its recruitment campaign.

Kitchener was a successful field commander but he liked autonomy and abhorred red tape and this did not make him popular with many of his contemporaries and his appointment as Secretary of State for War was not popular with some of the senior British Army staff officers, who proved awkward and in some cases deliberately obstructive to his plans to expand the Army. Kitchener had never liked the Territorial Force either, describing it as 'unwieldy.' He had been opposed to its creation in 1908 and was not prepared to use its framework for his expansion plans. Kitchener wanted to raise completely new armies; malleable, untainted by old military doggerel, they would be 'Kitchener's Armies.' He believed the country should prepare itself for at least a period of three years of conflict that would require some seventy divisions to fight it. The men he would wish to call upon would all be volunteers, each enlisting as regular soldiers for three years or the duration of the war, who would also commit to serve anywhere, home or abroad. Consequently, on the same day that he formally assumed his duties as Secretary of State for War, Kitchener presented his request to raise an army of 500,000 men to Parliament. His request was granted and the first adverts appealing for his first 100,000 men started to appear in newspapers and on posters soon afterwards.

Did you know?

The iconic Kitchener poster depicting the man himself with his pointing finger was used far less than popularly believed; instead his face and call for volunteers appeared in magazines, on postcards and all manner of badges and promotional items.

Recruiting offices were set up and opened their doors to receive the first volunteers for the 'New Army' on 11 August 1914 and on that same day Kitchener's famous call to arms 'Your King and Country Need You' was first published, calling for 100,000 men between the

Above left: 'If the Cap fits YOU join the Army today' recruiting poster published by the Parliamentary Recruiting Committee, 1915. (Library of Congress)
Above right: 'There is still a place in the line for YOU. Will you fill it?' published by the Parliamentary Recruiting Committee, February 1915. (Library of Congress)
Left: 'Another Call for More Men' published by the Parliamentary Recruiting Committee, December 1914.

ages of nineteen and thirty to enlist, ex-soldiers were accepted up to the age of forty-five. Local newspapers also ran the adverts publishing lists of the places where men could enlist. The appeal was met with patriotic zeal: recruitment drives were held in every town, public meetings were held with local dignitaries, clergy and military officers delivering speeches voicing 'appeals to patriotism,' military bands would fill market places with music, flags and bunting would be put out. The pressure was on, the generation targeted had been instilled with sense of duty to 'King and Country.' Posters called out 'Your Country Needs You' to help defend Britain and all it stood for from 'the marauding Huns.' Other posters questioned men's motives for not joining up, quoting Kitchener: 'Make sure your reason for not joining is not a feeble excuse.' Young women were also asked to consider 'Why is *your* boy not in khaki?' Such appeals to patriotism saw groups of young girls arm themselves with white feathers, which could be presented to any man not thought to be 'doing his bit.'

Boys too young and men over the age limit altered their birth certificates so they could enlist. Well-built lads presenting themselves to Recruiting Sergeants would be asked their age, some said sixteen, the old Sergeant would weigh the lad up and if he looked sizeable to pass muster he would be told to 'go out, come back in and tell me different'. Outside the door would be a few chaps in uniform who would 'put the boy right,' he would return, tell the Sergeant he was nineteen and he would be signed up for active service. By 21 August 1914 Kitchener had received his first 100,000 recruits and what became known as 'K1', the first six divisions of the 'New Army', was approved by the War Office. In total, there were to be five 'New Armies' formed under the Kitchener scheme; this meant most line infantry regiments received about three battalions of the New Army some, such as the Northumberland Fusiliers, Royal Fusiliers, the Middlesex or the Manchester Regiment had many more. Once adopted by their regiment the new units became known as Service Battalions.

Did you know?

Even after all they had gone through and into extreme old age many of those who had answered the call as volunteers would say with some pride that they had been 'Kitchener Men.'

Recruitment literature plainly laid out the terms; on enlistment, a man would receive 7*s* a week, emphasising food and clothing (the poster did not immediately say uniform) were included. Separation allowances granted the wife of a soldier with no children 12*s* 6*d* per week, with one child 15*s*, two children 17*s* 6*d*, three children 20*s*, four children 22*s* and an additional 2*s* per child if they had more than four. A promise was also made – 'Provided the Soldier does his share, the Government will assist liberally in keeping up, within the limits of separation allowance for families, any regular contribution made before enlistment by unmarried soldiers or widowers to other dependants such as mothers, fathers sisters etc.' Motherless children were granted 3*s* a week each, exclusive of allotment from the soldier's pay.

Pay was the deciding factor for recruitment in some country areas. August was harvest month, war or no war, and it was the best money an agricultural labourer could earn all year (about 21*s* a week, three times Army basic pay) and with the Territorials called up many

Men of Kitchener's Army on the march, 1914.

No. 1 Platoon, B Company, 11th (Service) Battalion, East Lancashire Regiment, 'The Accrington Pals', 1914.

farms were shorthanded. Young men in the towns were under serious pressure to enlist, whereas the more sparsely populated country areas saw many country lads hold off just long enough for a few weeks' harvesting and then join up.

From late August 1914, the emphasis was on friends joining together, be they from sports teams, work colleagues, old boys of a particular school or lads from a particular area of a city, town or village. In Northern cities such as Sheffield, Salford, Accrington, Leeds and Durham the units raised were known as 'Pals Battalions.' September 1914 saw the recruitment drives intensify; the harvest had been gathered in, and efforts were redoubled in more industrial areas.

Did you know?

Sportsmen were highly desirable candidates for recruitment, professionals left their clubs to join and entire amateur teams were known to patriotically join together.

An appeal from the government for independent civilian bodies to raise and fund units for the New Army (the monies would be refunded when the units were adopted by the War Office) met with great success; the first of these was raised by the Newcastle and Gateshead Chamber of Commerce, completed in less than a week, registered and acknowledged by the War Office on 16 September 1914. The 'Newcastle Commercials' went on to become 16th (Service) Battalion, Northumberland Fusiliers. The Scottish and Irish communities of a number of big cities formed the nucleus of more units such as the Liverpool Scottish, Tyneside Scottish and the Tyneside Irish. Many of these units appealed to those who were not part of the Scottish or Irish communities who joined with their friends and fancied the 'crack' of wearing a kilt and marching to bagpipes. The War Office was not so keen on this idea and the soldiers of these units had to accept the concession of only being permitted to wear Scottish headdress, such as glengarries or Tam o' Shanters.

New recruits for Kitchener's Army doing Swedish Drill exercises in a public park, 1914.

Above left: An appeal for sportsmen to come and 'do their bit'. Published by the Publicity Department, Central London Recruitment Depot, Whitehall, London, 1915.
Above right: Recruiting Poster for the Tyneside Scottish, designed and printed by Andrew Reid Printers of Newcastle, 1914.

During the month of September 1914, an average of 33,000 volunteers were enlisting on a daily basis. As far as supplies went, officers were fortunate; although they had to buy their own uniform and personal equipment, there were plenty of local tailors and national companies such as Army & Navy Stores who had bolts of green serge, barathea and similar quality cloth in various shades of khaki and green to supply the needs of newly enlisted subalterns.

Not every man who was eligible or of ability to obtain a commission did so. Many of the officer corps had public school backgrounds and some of them elected to start exclusive public-school battalions. Others were quite happy to serve among the rank and file but their manners and speech often set them apart as what became known as 'Gentlemen rankers'. They often made good NCO material and can be seen in uniformed studio portraits affecting the handkerchief tucked up their sleeve and partially revealed at the cuff, as well as having little nuances tolerated, such as private-purchase leather gloves. Many a promising young man was also lost to the officer corps in the early years of the war because all officers' uniform and equipment had to be privately purchased and the jacket alone could cost the equivalent of a month's wages to a working man. If a boy had received a scholarship to attend a grammar school, or his parents had scraped money together to pay for him to go to university and he was just starting out in life, neither he

Above: Newly commissioned line infantry subalterns from Cambridge University Officer Training Corps, Cambridge, 1914. **Right**: Price list for officer's uniform and equipment, 1915. Such costs were often beyond the means of educated working class men until the government provided a subsidy.

nor his family could afford the uniform. The problem was recognised and a grant was established for prospective officers who required it.

Meanwhile, as thousands flocked to join up, the supply of uniforms and equipment for soldiers rapidly ran out and the newly enlisted rank and file recruits of the New Army (and many Territorial Force Reserve Battalions) began their basic training in their own clothes and boots with only armbands, lanyards, and improvised or locally produced unofficial badges to signify he was 'doing his bit.'

When supplies of uniforms of kit arrived, they came piecemeal. Quartermasters were often seen red-faced and frustrated,

Above left: A sergeant and 'Gentleman Ranker', 6th (Service) Battalion, Royal Berkshire Regiment, 1916.
Above right: With stocks depleted and suppliers under pressure, uniforms came through piecemeal for Kitchener's Army, and the postcard cartoonists satirised the time well.

scratching their heads after the weekly delivery of odd items of uniform – jackets for three men, caps for five, puttees for ten, for example, accompanied by an assortment of webbing equipment such as a crate of fifty pouches but no belts or cross-straps to attach them to. Even things as basic as knife, fork and spoon sets had to be shared. Factories were at maximum output; most took on more staff and worked shifts around the clock. A new type of webbing equipment made simply in leather with brass fittings was brought in as an emergency measure in 1914; by 1915 tunics were being made without details such as pleats in the pockets, but still the supplies struggled to meet demand.

The lack of uniform did not stop basic training; the men were told to wear their working clothes and they were put through their paces in drill, rifle training and physical exercise, but it was not without formal complaints being made for compensation for wear and tear of privately owned clothes and especially boots. Out of desperation the War Office introduced 'The Kitchener Blue' – probably the most disliked uniform in the history of the British Army. The jackets and trousers were sourced from pre-war uniform stocks held for postmen, prison warders and prisoners (the uniforms for prisoners tended to be grey and had to be dyed for Army use). The Army looked to its stores and found its only major stockpiles of equipment was the pre-1900 Slade-Wallace and Valise pattern (the classic whitened hide pouches, belts and cross straps worn in during the reign of Queen Victoria). The trouble was the soldiers did

Soldiers from a Northamptonshire Regiment Service Battalion wearing 'Kitchener Blue' uniforms and a motley selection of cap badges and insignia, 1914.

No. 10 Platoon, C Company, 16th (Service) Battalion, West Yorkshire Regiment, 'The Bradford Pals', 1914. The officers wear their private-purchase service dress and the men have a smart turnout in their 'Kitchener Blue' uniforms. (Courtesy of Mark Davis)

not have the pipe clay to re-whiten their grubby old equipment; mind you there wasn't much of it to go around so most men ended up wearing a belt and just one ammunition pouch. This Victorian webbing was accompanied with an issue of rifles of similar vintage and when these ran out the men were issued with wooden 'dummy' rifles and even broomsticks to practice their drill. The uniform was crowned with a side cap of simple construction.

The public didn't know what to make of these strange blue uniforms. Comments were made that 'prison warders' had been conscripted to maintain order; some even though they were Belgian refugee soldiers. There were still not enough military buttons and regimental badges to go around, and even when khaki uniforms became more plentiful men still ended up wearing collar badges or even buttons in their hats in place of a cap badge. To cap it all off, much of the dyeing of the uniforms had been done in haste and the dyes ran if the uniform

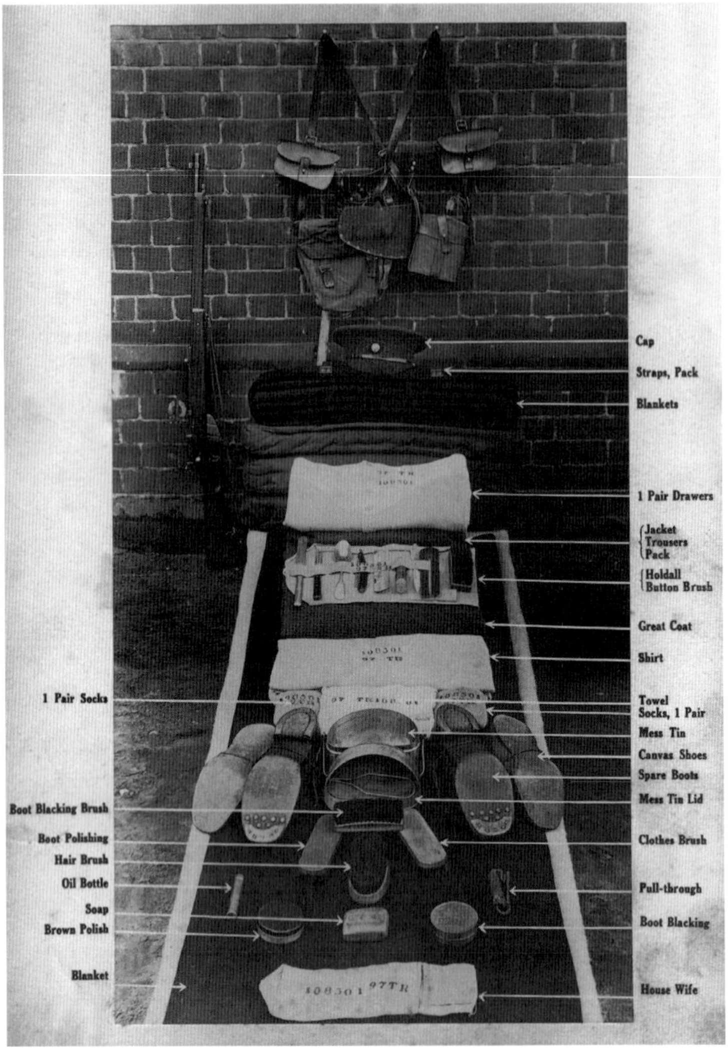

Instructional photograph used by a Training Reserve battalion to show recruits how their kit, equipment and spare uniform items should be laid out for inspection, 1916.

got wet or sweaty, turning the soldier's skin blue. In typical good humour, the Service Battalion soldiers invented their own song about their tribulations featuring Fred Karno, who was in those days 'King of the Comedians'. There are various versions – this is the cleanest:

We are Fred Karno's Army,
Fred Karno's infantry,
We cannot fight, we cannot shoot,
What God damn use are we?
But when we get to Berlin,
The Kaiser he will say,
Hoch, Hoch, Mein Gott!
What a bloomin' fine lot,
Fred Karno's sent today!

Above left: Regimental Sergeant Major, Durham Light Infantry, 1915.
Above right: Seaside comic postcard artist Donald McGill satirises the bawling sergeants that trained the men of Kitchener's Army, 1914.
Right: The feeling experienced by many a Kitchener volunteer after a route march, 1914.

In total, there were to be five 'New Armies', the last formed under authorisation in March 1915. The backbones of the fourth and fifth New Armies were to be the groups of soldiers raised in cities and large towns, many of them from the industrial North known unofficially as 'Pals' or 'Chums' Battalions. The first of the 'Kitchener Battalions' proceeded to France and Flanders in May 1915.

Training in trench warfare under battle conditions began when they arrived. Each unit would spend about a month in training. Under the supervision of bawling sergeant instructors, the men charged their sacks of hay hung from gallows and stuck their bayonets

Talented cartoonist Fergus Mackain served in 23rd (Service) Battalion, Royal Fusiliers, and drew on his own experiences to produce a series of poignant postcards reflecting army life from training to the front line.

in key points marked on the bag, fired at targets with the faces of German soldiers printed on them, and some took on specialities such as sniping, advanced signalling, trench mortars and grenade 'bombing'. They were all expected to train in digging and maintaining trenches under fire.

Did you know?

Kitchener never got to see his army in any major action. When many of his battalions were decimated on the Somme he was already dead. While travelling on a diplomatic mission to Russia, Kitchener's ship, HMS *Hampshire,* stuck a mine and sank with the loss of most of her crew, including Kitchener, on 5 June 1916. His body was never recovered.

Kitchener's Army had been an unprecedented success but the Army still needed more men. The Derby Scheme, named after Edward Stanley, 17th Early of Derby – Kitchener's new Director General of Recruiting – urged men to come forward voluntarily to register and be sworn in. Each man who had been found fit and had undertaken the obligation was then transferred to the Army Reserve to await call up and was issued with a 'Derby Scheme' khaki armband with a scarlet crown to signify this.

Uptake for the scheme was not as good as hoped and the government felt it could no longer depend solely on the recruitment of volunteers. Conscription was therefore

Above: Soldiers training in the use of the bayonet, c. 1915.
Right: Gale and Polden instructional card showing how the sacks charged at in training related to the enemy, 1915.

proposed by the government as a measure to meet this need. The Military Service Act, which made all men between the ages of eighteen and forty-one liable for military service (unless they were in a war reserved occupation, married, widowed with children or a minister of religion), was introduced in January 1916 and came into force on 2 March 1916. A second Act of May 1916 extended the Act to include married men and the third Act in 1918 raised the age limit to fifty-one. Individual men or their employers could object to their conscription by making an application for an exemption to their local Military Service Tribunal.

Above: One of the armbands issued to Derby Scheme volunteers, 1915.
Left: The cover of *The War Budget*, Christmas 1914.

4
On Active Service

The British Expeditionary Force (BEF), consisting of 100,000 men in six infantry divisions and five cavalry brigades, began embarkation for France on 9 August 1914. Mobilisation had gone smoothly but not without problems. Horses had to be loaded into the holds of troopships using cranes and cargo nets and some of them died of shock in the process. The troopships were so packed there was only standing room on many of them and the rough crossings combined with the fact that some of the vessels had been cattle boats and still carried the stench of animal excrement, mixed with the sickness and upset stomachs of men and horses, meant that many soldiers suffered terrible sea sickness during their crossing. Some of the BEF units were fortunate enough to have a brief crossing from Dover to Calais or Boulogne while others had longer journeys to Le Havre or Rouen followed by a slow and uncomfortable journey by train, travelling in cattle trucks to their battalion's assembly area. The BEF assembled as a whole at its concentration point of Mauberge by 20 August 1914.

At this point it is worth exploring the command structure of an infantry division in the First World War. Most infantry divisions would be led by a lieutenant general or major-general and would contain a mix of corps and infantry personnel with total strength of about 598 officers and 18,077 NCOs and men. Within the division there would normally be three brigades, under the command of a brigadier-general; brigades were made up of four battalions of line infantry with 800 to 1,000 men in each battalion. Each battalion was headed by the OC (Officer Commanding), normally a lieutenant-colonel, and comprised HQ Company (OC, Adjutant, clerks, quartermaster, signallers, drivers etc.) and then four rifle companies, normally named 'A', 'B', 'C' and 'D', each commanded by a major. Each rifle company consisted of 240 NCOs and men, each divided into four platoons of sixty men. Infantry platoons were then divided into sections led by an NCO.

Shortly after their arrival, BEF reconnaissance parties had been spotted by German troops who reported seeing 'Dun (brown) clothed golfers' – the tall puttees and trouser combination with rifles looked like a golfer in his plus fours carrying his clubs at a distance. The Kaiser himself, it was claimed in a report widely published in the British press, referred to the BEF as 'General French's contemptible little Army.' Despite the report being proved to be more propaganda than fact, the name stuck, and the men of the BEF became rather proud of it – they even named their old comrades association 'The Old Contemptibles'.

On 23 August 1914, the BEF was engaged in its first major action at Mons. They fought bravely; the enemy believed they were facing machine-gun fire when in fact they were encountering the rapid fire of rifles in the hands of trained regular British soldiers. However, the numbers of German troops and the sudden retreat of the French 5th Army exposed the British flank and left them with no other option than to undertake a tactical withdrawal, which soon turned into a fighting retreat. A stop line had to be drawn up as the threat to Paris increased and the Battle of the Marne (7–12 September 1914) proved a success for the Allies. French Commander in Chief Joffre gave the order to entrench and the Allies dug trenches so they could maintain a firm defensive stand. The Germans followed suit but neither side could find

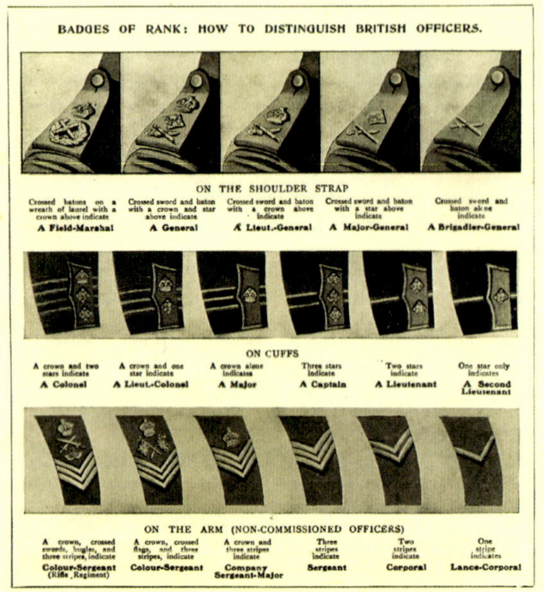

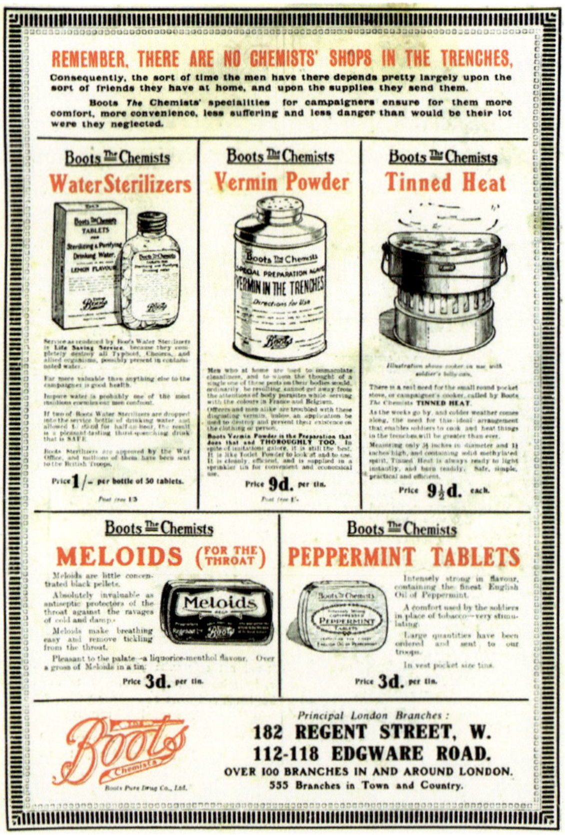

Above left: British Army badges of rank from lance-corporal to field marshal, 1914.

Above right: A French postcard showing soldiers of the British Expeditionary Force shortly after their arrival in France, 1914.

Left: The requisites of Tommies they asked to be sent out to them from their families at home were soon picked up on by enterprising business like Boots, the chemist, who were soon advertising a range of products to make life in the trenches more comfortable.

a way to break the deadlock as each side raced for the sea and the vital supply lines ports could provide for such a war. By Christmas 1914 the trench lines of the Western Front extended for some 440 miles from the Belgian coast to the neutral Swiss border. The British were designated to hold 85 miles of front line between Ypres and the Somme. It was during this first bitterly cold Christmas that very unofficial truces broke out between the lines of the British and the German forces near Ploegsteert, Belgium – or 'Plug Street', as the soldiers called it.

Among them were the men of 1st Battalion, the Norfolk Regiment, including Pte. Bertie Guymer who gave an interview three months later when he was returned wounded:

> At 10.00 p.m. on Christmas Eve the Germans got up on top of their trenches. One man called out "Don't fire, I want to talk." He walked half way to our trench and "Cock" Warminger, the heavy-weight boxer of Norwich, left our trench and met him. The two men shook hands and exchanged presents of cigars and chocolates. The men returned to their respective trenches, and then the Germans came out, having left their rifles behind. We joined them and there was a sing along. We gave them *Tipperary* and they responded with *The Watch of the Rhine*. We buried some dead Frenchmen, Germans and Norfolks digging the graves, and a German officer read the prayers. After that we walked about as we liked and were glad to do so as there was a sharp frost. Our officers cut off their buttons and exchanged them for the German officer's buttons. The Germans told us they kept Christmas for three days and during that period not a shot was fired.

These truces did not go down well with those higher up the command structure and the troops involved were reprimanded and removed from the line, but not before New Year when many from both sides risked one more night of peace and even some more fraternisation.

The battle lines created in 1914 remained more or less intact for the next four years. Despite all the pushes, counter attacks, raids, advances and retreats on both sides, the Western Front not only kept a similar line, it was fought over a width of just 4 miles – no wonder many parts of this front line soon looked like a muddy surface of the moon pockmarked by the shell craters of artillery and mortar rounds.

The trench system favoured by the British consisted of three lines of trenches: the front line, support, and reserve with barbed wire entanglements in front. Beyond that was 'No Man's Land' that allowed a distance of anything between 25 yards and half a mile between British lines and the enemy (the average was around 250 yards).

The Princess Mary Gift Tin, 1914. The tins sent to soldiers in France usually contained a packet of cigarettes and a packet of tobacco, accompanied by a Christmas card, a greetings card from King George V and Queen Mary, and a portrait card of the young princess.

Some of the lads of the London Rifle Brigade in the trenches during the winter, 1915–16.

Pte. Frederick William Heath of 1/13th (County of London) Battalion, the London Regiment, wrote home with an evocative account of daily life in a front-line trench during the winter of 1914–15:

> The weather is causing a good deal of trouble at present. We first get snow and frost, then a quick thaw, then another snap of frost, with bitter cold winds and perhaps rain. The effect of this on the trenches has been vile. When I was last in them four days ago, we were up to the calves in mud. Imagine me pushing my way through this with full pack and rifle until I get to my appointed post! Here I stick with my rifle, with bayonet fixed, through a loop hole cut out of earth heaped on top of the trench and stand on observation duty for two, four and six hours, as the case may be.
>
> Generally it is two hours on and two hours off. When you are on, you have to keep your eye glued to the loophole and endeavour to spot any movement of men in the German trenches, the first of which is only 100 yards away from our trench. For the past week the enemy has been sapping right up to our trenches and it is believed that he is preparing some mine scheme to blow us out!
>
> We see very little during the day, but at night those of us whose nerves are not good see a great deal. When I am off duty I crawl into a hole cut in the side of the trench and doubling myself up, pull a waterproof sheet – the soldier's best friend in the trenches – over me and try to snatch a little sleep. And so the night goes on. Comes the hour before daybreak, when we all stand to arms.
>
> As soon as it is light, we get our fires going and begin to cook breakfast. Here is a typical day's menu:-

Soldiers spending day after day in a filthy trench with no chance of a good wash soon became infested with lice.

I've got a chum in my company who sticks to me closer than a brother!

> Breakfast – Bacon fried in our mess tin lids, bread roasted in the bacon fat, jam, butter, tea.
>
> Dinner – Corned beef, cold or hot as you like; biscuits, bread and cheese, varied by camp ration containing tinned meat and vegetables.
>
> Tea – Bread, butter and jam.
>
> Of course many of us take up little luxuries of our own. But you will see how wonderfully fed we are. Then about eleven o'clock at night there is the rum parade. Neat rum it is and by Jove! How we long for it! Of course, this will go on only so long as our transport can come up to the trenches. As things are at present, the transport halts in a ruined village only a couple of hundred yards behind our trenches. A ration party of about twenty men is detailed shortly after dusk and goes out to the transport and brings back the rations. It runs the risk of snipers, but one gets used to that.

Unlike the French who left divisions of troops in the front line until they suffered such casualties they were replaced by another division, and suffered terrible morale as a result, the British infantry battalions at the front were rotated. Battalions would begin their time in the support lines for a week then had a week on the front line. Time could be extended – sometimes a double stint 'in the line' could be requested, but it was rare for any British unit to regularly do more than ten days on the front line. When relieved by the next unit to take over their position, the departing battalions would have six days 'out of the line' at 'rest camp', where first and foremost the men could access showers or baths to get clean and have their uniforms de-loused.

Did you know?

Soldiers made light of lice and did their best by 'chatting' out the eggs by drawing the seams of their clothes where the eggs collected over a candle flame. As they did so they talked to each other and a new term entered British parlance. So next time you have a 'chat'...

Next, they would try to get a pass to visit a nearby village and one of the little estaminets where there was usually a good egg and chips on offer with a glass of wine for a franc or two. There was often a YMCA or similar canteen 'hut' at the rest camp, or not too far away, where a soldier could write a proper letter home on the paper provided for free, buy postcards to write home, have a warm drink and buy a snack such as a few biscuits or even a chocolate bar.

Rest camps, however, were frequently far from restful as the military like to make sure their soldiers were kept occupied. They were expected to parade, had to smarten their uniforms, maintain their kit, polish buttons, do drill, take part in exercises and get roped into camp maintenance and chores. If the workload of nearby pioneer battalions was stretching them, the rest camp soldiers would be called to help out as they made and remade roads, laid railways and dug trenches. Some lads joked they went back to the front line for a bit of peace and quiet.

Although some British infantry battalions kept up the offensive against the enemy with regular trench raids, large stretches of the front line were so close that grenades or mortar fire could easily be exchanged regularly. This achieved nothing but more death, so long stretches of the line rapidly fell into a 'live and let live' way of life where if one side did not bomb the other they would not reply in kind unless they were under orders. In some places firing stopped during certain times of the day so that the likes of water carrying parties could make easier journeys without being shot at.

Attempts were made to break the deadlock of the trenches; battles like Neuve-Chappelle (10–13 March 1915) Battle of Loos (25 September–13 October 1915) where poison gas was unleashed by the Germans upon British forces for the first time and the First Battle of Ypres (19 October–22 November 1915) cost thousands of lives, but strategically very little was achieved.

British Tommies make friends with the 'Madame' of their local estaminet, 1916.

Above left: Always a handy thing when trying to communicate with allies and locals alike, a *6d* French phrase book and handmade cover to protect it, *c.* 1916.

Above right: Cameron Highlanders, not long out of the trenches, 1916. French photographers often set up temporary 'studios' in the gardens and side streets (note the cobbled street, poorly fixed background drape) in villages close to rest camps to take souvenir photographs for troops to send home to family and friends.

Right: Magazines in Britain often had cover artwork showing an artist's impression of the latest brave deeds on the battlefronts This cover depicts L.Cpl. Leonard Keyworth, 24th (County of London) Battalion, the London Regiment, winning the Victoria Cross at Givenchy on the night of 25-26 May 1915. Five months later Leonard was killed in action. He was twenty-two years old.

Did you know?

In 1915 the First World War expanded to become a truly global conflict with the British Army engaged in major new campaigns in Mesopotamia and Gallipoli against the Ottoman Turkish Army. These campaigns cost thousands of lives and are often referred to in military histories as 'side shows'.

In December 1915, the senior Allied commanders on the Western Front gathered at Chantilly to discuss how to break out of the stalemate of the trenches. The French Army commander proposed that the planned new offensives on the Western Front should be delivered in different locations, but within a month of each other, so that the enemy were unable to move their reserves from one area of front to another in time to counter those attacks.

The French would attack at Verdun and the British on the Somme. After months of routine in the trenches of the Western Front suffering bitter cold, wet, mud, bodily infestations such as lice, losing mates to trench fever, trench foot, sickness, drop shorts (shells aimed at the enemy that didn't reach their trenches, 'dropping short' on British lines instead), snipers, raiding parties or just plain bad luck, many of the men on the Western Front were clamouring for a 'Big Push' and a chance to really get to grips with the enemy at last to do something that would break the deadlock of the trenches and get the war over with once and for all. On that bright sunny morning of 1 July 1916, they went bravely 'over the top' and were met by a hail of German bullets. Some Divisions, like the 18th (Eastern) Division at Montauban achieved their

Soldiers of a Queen's Regiment Service Battalion, still proudly wearing the leather webbing that was often retained by Kitchener battalions as a mark of distinction for their active service. On its reverse is a simple ink annotation - 'Somewhere in France, 1916'.

Above: Men of 4th Battalion, Worcestershire Regiment (a pre-war Regular Army battalion), marching towards the trenches at Acheux, Somme, France on 28 June 1916. One of them holds a large mallet aloft that would have been used to drive in heavy upright stakes during the construction and maintenance of trenches and trench defences. On 1 July 1916 they attacked Beaumont Hamel.
Right: Hudson trench whistle dated 1916. Whistles were used to signal attacks because they were one of the few sounds that could be reliably heard amidst gunfire and artillery barrage.

Soldiers going 'Over the Top,' during an attack on the Somme front, 1916. (Brown Family Collection)

objectives; others, such as the 34th Division, containing the Tyneside Scottish and Tyneside Irish brigades, attacked La Boiselle and sustained such casualties that even though some of the men got through to their objective, there were too few of them to hold it. The Tyneside Scottish and Irish brigades suffered the worst losses of any brigades on the First Day of the Somme.

Private Robert Walker of the Tyneside Scottish was one of those wounded in the attack and wrote home to his wife from his hospital bed:

> We had been in the trenches for 14 days, and we should have made our attack on the 29th June, but it was put off till the morning of July 1st. Well, we took up our position at 2 o'clock in the morning. We were up to the knees in mud and water. We got a tot of rum and a drop of cold tea, but it was awfully cold tea, and we had not to make the attack till 7.30. At 6 o'clock we started to shell the German first line trench. This put the Germans on their guard, because they knew we were coming. It fell to the luck of the Tyneside Scottish to lead the charge of the Division. The Tyneside Irish had to follow us. Now 7.30 came, and over we went with the pipers playing. We had about 600 yards to go for the first line of the German trenches, but as soon as we showed our heads the German machine guns started, and hundreds of our men were shot down before we got away from our own trenches. The shots were striking the ground the same as you see a heavy fall of hailstones. It was then I hardly knew how I was doing it, but I kept my eyes off those that were falling in case I saw anybody I knew, for if I had it might have affected my spirits, so on I went...

A total of 60,000 soldiers were killed or wounded on the first day, but the Battles of the Somme went on until 18 November 1916; overall, 420,000 British casualties were sustained in the Somme battles. Although not much ground was gained, the British Army had not lost any ground either, and over the course of the battle had inflicted heavy casualties on the enemy and taken thousands as prisoners of war.

The year 1917 saw renewed attacks in the Ypres sector in the muddy and bloody battles of Arras and Passchendaele (The Third Battle of Ypres, 31 July–10 November 1917), where at the latter it is estimated the British Army suffered 260,000 casualties.

Tommies going up the line passing a row of German prisoners being taken to a holding camp, Somme front, 1916.

Did you know?

The year 1917 also saw a new theatre of war open in Palestine. British troops crossed the Sinai Desert and advanced on Gaza. After two costly battles to take the city a new commander, Edmund Allenby, was brought in. He used a different strategy, changing the face of the war in the Holy Land and taking Jerusalem by Christmas. This victory gave great hope to the Allies the world over.

By late 1917 warfare and weaponry were changing on the Western Front. British infantry battalions were being supplied with more portable machine guns (Lewis Guns) that although heavy, could be picked up by one man and used against the enemy. They were also being supplied with the more reliable Mills Grenades, so useful for clearing German bunkers when occupying enemy trenches. Aerial reconnaissance provided valuable information about enemy positions and the accuracy of the gunnery of artillery was improved as a result. Although they still had teething problems, tanks were great for morale, more troops were arriving from the British Empire and Commonwealth, and the American Expeditionary Force had begun to arrive in France. The war was becoming more mobile again.

Hopes had been high among the British that there may be an end to the war over the winter of 1917–18, but under the pressure of a war of attrition the German Army made one final gamble for victory with a spring offensive in 1918, otherwise known as the *Kaiserschlact* (The Kaiser's Battle). Beginning on 21 March 1918, the German forces wrong-footed the Allies and soon achieved one of the deepest advances by either side since 1914.

Prisoners of War

Prisoners of war (POWs) are often forgotten in the story of the First World War. Over 181,000 officers and men of the British Army ended up in German captivity during the conflict. There were some camps in occupied France and Belgium but the majority were in Germany. Early POW camps were little more than barbed wire corrals with no covered shelter where soldiers were held under armed guard and left to fend for themselves regardless of rain, wind or snow. Tents followed and straw was provided for the men to sleep on. Eventually the materials for barrack huts were supplied and the prisoners were set to work building them. It was then quite a while before stoves were supplied to heat them and washing facilities were often no more than a cold water pump. Living conditions did improve in time; prison uniforms were supplied and soldiers were allowed to have concerts to raise their morale, but the lack of food remained a problem, especially when the prisoners were expected to spend the day labouring on nearby farms, carrying sacks in granaries, felling trees in forests, building roads, laying railway tracks or even working down mines. Pte L. Lawn, who was held at Sennelager POW Camp, described his diet:

> Our food for the day was a pint of coffee for breakfast with nothing to eat, dinner about a pint and a half of soup. We used to march round big coppers with a tin basin and got it ladled out as we went past. If we were caught going twice we got tied up or our bread stopped. For tea we got a slice of bread each or they gave us a loaf to cut up, ten men to a 4 lb loaf. Sometimes we got a raw herring or a piece of sausage to eat with it.

The lives of our POWs were greatly helped by the Red Cross, who inspected camps, supplied food parcels to supplement their meagre diet, and provided some comforts such as books and musical instruments. Great efforts were undertaken back in Britain by regimental and organised civilian groups who set up county prisoner of war support groups to raise money to send tinned food, cakes and comforts to their men in captivity.

'London Boys' among the British soldiers held as prisoners of war at the Rennbahn POW Camp, Germany, 1917. Some of these men are still wearing their khaki uniforms while others wear the dark navy blue jackets and trousers with brown stripes issued to British soldier prisoners of war.

Above left: British prisoners of war from Doeberitz POW Camp, Germany, at work under armed guard, *c.* 1915.
Above right: A prisoner of war from the Manchester Regiment. Note his prison camp and personal prisoner number patched onto the front of his jacket, *c.* 1917.
Below left: Letter with a facsimile message from King George V welcoming British prisoners of war back from captivity.
Below right: The advertisers in *The War Budget* suggest a few things to send to prisoners of war in Germany, 1915.

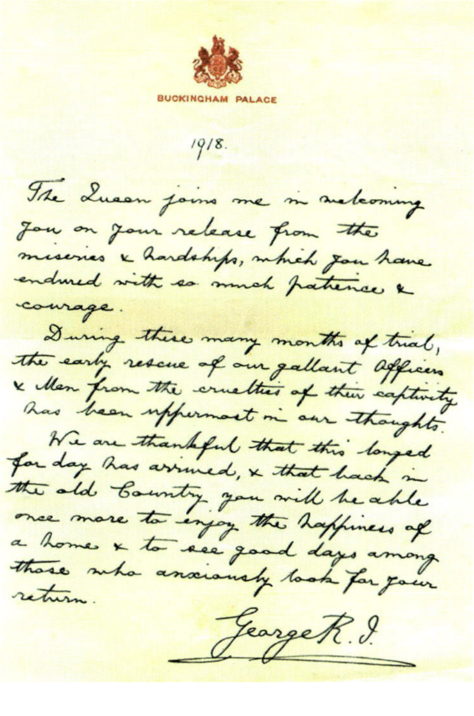

BUCKINGHAM PALACE

1918.

The Queen joins me in welcoming you on your release from the miseries & hardships, which you have endured with so much patience & courage.

During these many months of trial, the early rescue of our gallant Officers & Men from the cruelties of their captivity has been uppermost in our thoughts.

We are thankful that this longed for day has arrived, & that back in the old Country you will be able once more to enjoy the happiness of a home & to see good days among those who anxiously look for your return.

George R. I.

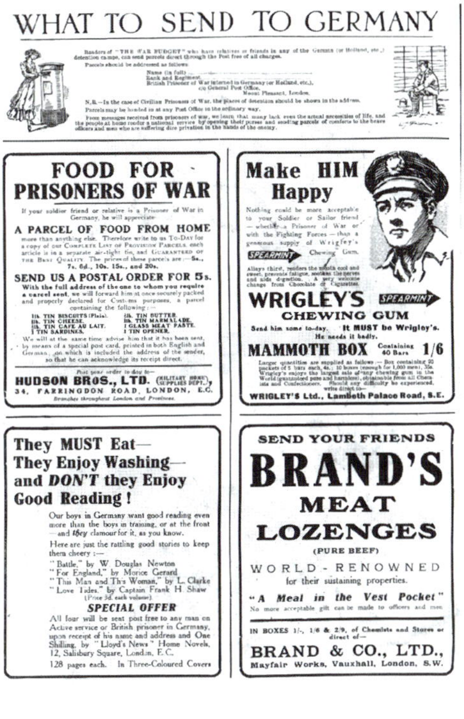

WHAT TO SEND TO GERMANY

Readers of "THE WAR BUDGET" who have relatives or friends in any of the German (or Holland, etc.) detention camps, can send parcels direct through the Post free of all charges.

Parcels should be addressed as follows:

Name (in full) ____
Rank and Regiment ____
British Prisoner of War interned in Germany (or Holland, etc.),
c/o General Post Office,
Mount Pleasant, London.

N.B.—In the case of Civilian Prisoners of War, the places of detention should be shown in the address.

Parcels may be handed in at any Post Office in the ordinary way.

From messages received from prisoners of war, we learn that many lack even the actual necessities of life, and the people at home render a national service by opening their purses and sending parcels of comforts to the brave officers and men who are suffering dire privation in the hands of the enemy.

FOOD FOR PRISONERS OF WAR

If your soldier friend or relative is a Prisoner of War in Germany, he will appreciate

A PARCEL OF FOOD FROM HOME

more than anything else. Therefore write to us TO-DAY for a copy of our COMPLETE LIST OF PROVISION PARCELS, each article is in a separate air-tight tin, and GUARANTEED OF THE BEST QUALITY. The prices of these parcels are:—5s., 7s. 6d., 10s. 15s., and 20s.

SEND US A POSTAL ORDER FOR 5s.

With the full address of the one to whom you require a parcel sent, we will forward him at once securely packed and properly declared for Customs purposes, a parcel containing the following:—

1lb. TIN BISCUITS (Plain). ½lb. TIN BUTTER.
½lb. TIN CHEESE. 1lb. TIN MARMALADE.
½lb. TIN CAFE AU LAIT. 1 GLASS MEAT PASTE.
1 TIN SARDINES. 1 TIN OPENER.

We will at the same time advise him that it has been sent, by means of a special post card, printed in both English and German, on which is included the address of the sender, so that he can acknowledge its receipt direct.

Post your order to-day to—
HUDSON BROS., LTD. (MILITARY HOME SUPPLIES DEPT.),
34, FARRINGDON ROAD, LONDON, E.C.
Branches throughout London and Provinces.

Make HIM Happy

Nothing could be more acceptable to your Soldier or Sailor friend — whether a Prisoner of War or with the Fighting Forces — than a generous supply of Wrigley's SPEARMINT Chewing Gum.

Allays thirst, renders the mouth cool and sweet, prevents fatigue, soothes the nerves and aids digestion. A very welcome change from Chocolate or Cigarettes.

WRIGLEY'S SPEARMINT CHEWING GUM

Send him some to-day. It MUST be Wrigley's. He needs it badly.

MAMMOTH BOX Containing 40 Bars 1/6

Larger quantities are supplied as follows:— Box containing 20 packets of 5 bars each, 4s.; 10 boxes (enough for 1,000 men), 35s. Wrigley's enjoys the largest sale of any chewing gum in the World (guaranteed pure and harmless), obtainable from all Chemists and Confectioners. Should any difficulty be experienced, write direct to—
WRIGLEY'S Ltd., Lambeth Palace Road, S.E.

They MUST Eat—
They Enjoy Washing—
and *DON'T* they Enjoy Good Reading!

Our boys in Germany want good reading even more than the boys in training, or at the front —and *they* clamour for it, as you know.

Here are just the rattling good stories to keep them cheery:—
"Battle," by W. Douglas Newton
"For England," by Morice Gerard
"This Man and This Woman," by L. Clarke
"Love Tides," by Captain Frank H. Shaw
(Price 3d. each volume)

SPECIAL OFFER

All four will be sent post free to any man on Active service or British prisoner in Germany, upon receipt of his name and address and One Shilling, by "Lloyd's News" Home Novels, 12, Salisbury Square, London, E.C.
128 pages each. In Three-Coloured Covers

SEND YOUR FRIENDS
BRAND'S MEAT LOZENGES
(PURE BEEF)
WORLD-RENOWNED for their sustaining properties.
"*A Meal in the Vest Pocket*"
No more acceptable gift can be made to officers and men

IN BOXES 1/-, 1/6 & 2/9, of Chemists and Stores or direct of—
BRAND & CO., LTD.,
Mayfair Works, Vauxhall, London, S.W.

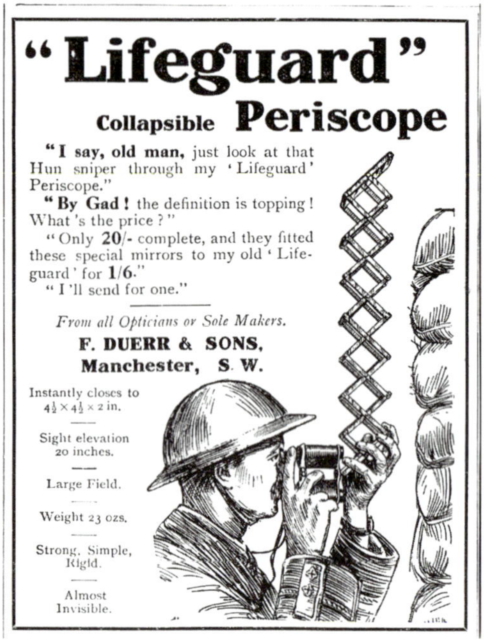

Above left: The observational humour of the trenches was captured in the enormously popular works of Captain Bruce Bairnsfather. Originally published in the *Bystander*, his cartoon were also published as postcards and number of *Fragments from France* compendiums of his cartoons were published during the war.

Above right: A number of articles were also developed specifically for trench warfare, notably periscopes to enable safe observation over the top of the trench.

Below: A typical mud-sodden trench in France, 1917.

Set of three Bamforth song cards for 'Take me Back to Dear Old Blighty.' First published in 1916, its catchy, sing-along tune made it one of the most popular and enduring songs of the First World War.

The Allies withdrew and concentrated their forces to essential areas such as the approach to channel ports and railway junctions leaving the war-torn battlefield areas that were of little or no tactical value only lightly defended. The German targets were often changed due to tactical situations on the battlefields and the German logistics supplying food, ammunition and men to the advance could not keep up with their fighting troops, the offensive could not be sustained and the main thrust of the *Kaiserschlact* had petered out by late April 1918. The danger of a German breakthrough had passed. Already having sustained horrific casualties, the German Army was knocked back by an Allied counteroffensive in August 1918 with the might of over a million men of the American Expeditionary Force fresh to the front to support it. So began the 'Hundred Days Offensive' with the Battle of Amiens on 8 August 1918. The tanks were in full force and combined with allied massive infantry assault this truly marked the end of the stagnation of trench warfare on the Western Front. Fighting was mobile again; German forces were driven or retreated from the ground they had taken during the spring offensive. The Hindenburg Line was a tough obstacle to crack but it was finally broken in September 1918. The days of war were then numbered.

Even though the hopes for an end to the war increased every day in November 1918, there had been a number of false alarms. When the news actually arrived and was confirmed and the cheering had died away, it left the fighting men with very surreal feelings.

Capt. Charles Cooke recorded that moment and his observations in *Historical Records of the 9th (Service) Battalion Northumberland Fusiliers*:

> The news of the Armistice came through to the men of 9th Battalion via a communiqué from 61st Division headquarters at 08.00 hours stating "Hostilities will cease 1100 hours to-day November 11th. Stand fast on line reached at that hour which will be reported by wire to Corps Headquarters. Defensive precautions will be maintained. There will be no intercourse of any description with the enemy. Ends."

A lone soldier stands sentry near the ruins of the Ypres Cloth Hall, 1918. (Brown Family Collection)

The men cheered and Lieutenant-Colonel Thomson spoke to the companies in turn, telling them to keep up the training. The Brigadier arrived and addresses the men in similar terms. Training then proceeded! Such was the reception of the news by a hard-fighting battalion, with all its honours fresh upon it. What a contrast to the wild scenes at home. It really took time for the significance of Armistice to be appreciated. No more shells, no more rifle-fire, no more gas, no more machine-guns, no more "over-the-top", no more ------ oh! All these things were finished. After more than three years of it, the "old hands" could scarcely realise the position. Immense silence followed the continual inferno of flame and noise. Eyes still shone with the strange light of perplexity, that far-away look of men who went through life expecting each moment to meet death. The everlasting nearness of the borderland, the feeling of its almost inevitability left their mark on the strained features. It is still there for thoughtful people to see – the mark that proclaims a Man.

Above: Soldiers on their transport ready to go to their rest camp after serving their term on a front line on the Somme, 1916. The battalion has clearly engaged with the enemy and are wearing a few war trophy hats.
Below: Stretcher bearers, having collected a wounded soldier from No Man's Land, head for the Regimental Aid Post, Passchendaele, 1917.

5
The Wounded

In the wars up to the First World War, the majority of deaths on foreign campaign service were due to disease not battle; this was a tragic but hardly surprising statistic when you consider our soldiers were serving across a vast Empire in many hot and sultry climes, from India to the West Indies, and the lack of the medicines and inoculations available to us in the modern world.

Did you know?

The First World War was the first war to use such weapons as heavy artillery and mines, machine guns, and poison gas on an unprecedented scale. As a result, the majority of casualties were sustained as a result of active service in the field.

The most common and consistent causes of injury and death in action came from artillery shell fire; thousands of men were simply blown to smithereens, caught by shrapnel or buried under the waves of mud thrown up by the explosive shells. The names of tens of thousands of men carved upon the Thiepval Memorial and the Menin Gate bear mute testimony to the missing who have no known grave. Then there were machine guns. If the enemy were able to position a pair of machine guns over an area and successfully achieve enfilading fire along the length of an attacking formation of troops the advancing soldiers were, as one German machine gunner recalled, 'mown down like corn in a field'.

The biggest killers of the war on all fronts, however, were silent ones, for there would be many more left wounded after a battle than killed in it. In those days before antibiotics and the terrible conditions of agricultural field mud contaminated with manure, rats and foul water, it was the infection and complications such as shock that came as a result of suffering these wounds that proved to be the killer. Consider also those who succumbed to diseases and sicknesses such as cholera, malaria and dysentery, which were especially prevalent in the Mesopotamia and Palestine campaigns. On the Western Front, medical conditions such as 'trench fever', brought on when the many lice bites suffered by soldiers from their infested clothing became infected, or 'trench foot', brought about by the wet, muddy and cold conditions the men were often exposed to and that, in severe cases, could result in blood poisoning and prove fatal, were prevalent. Add these together and the casualty toll was truly horrendous.

If a man was wounded in action and could not move he was in a very vulnerable position. Men would do all they could to crawl back to their lines, dragging their shattered limbs with them; otherwise they would have to lie there, shout, scream and wait for stretcher bearers. If the attack was successful and the objective was consolidated, the removal of casualties from the field could be carried out soon after. But if, as so often happened, the ground was not held and the attacking troops fell back to their own lines, and if they did not pick you up on the way back, you could be left there until stretcher bearers were allowed to collect you under a white flag of truce, or

Did you know?

Figures published at the end of the war stated British Army casualties as a result of enemy action and disease were 673,375 killed and missing and a further 1,643,469 wounded. These figures did not include the thousands of men suffering permanent and long-term mental illness, often branded 'shell shock' or 'neurasthenia', as a result of their active service.

you would sometimes have to wait hours until nightfall when they would crawl out under cover of darkness to recover the wounded. Treatment for wounds carried out by regimental stretcher-bearers and RAMC men on the battlefield was simple and mainly consisted of the application of a shell dressing bound onto the wound and removal to British lines as soon as possible.

There are many moving stories of how medics, stretcher bearers, padres and comrades came out under fire to carry their wounded mates back and harrowing tales of how men were known to be lying wounded out in No Man's Land for hours or even days because the best efforts of their pals to reach them had been constantly frustrated by the intensity of gunfire over the area. Sometimes when the pal was eventually reached it was too late or under such an intensity of artillery fire bodies could simply disappear. Even when taken up upon a stretcher it could

British and German soldiers receive treatment at a Forward Dressing Station on the Somme, 1916. (Brown Family Collection)

still be a 'long carry' often over at least a mile through regimental aid post, dressing station and eventually to the casualty clearing station. When the injured soldiers eventually arrived, if the casualties had been heavy, there would already be a number in front of him laid on stretchers or ground sheets awaiting attention from the surgeon. Many simply did not make it through.

Did you know?

Those who were patched up would hope to be adjudged by the surgeon to have sustained what became known as a 'Blighty Wound' – one that was not life threatening but enough to get you a few quiet months back home in a comfy war hospital.

Tens of thousands of servicemen who 'caught a Blighty' would be removed by hospital ship back to England and then on to a network of hospitals ready to receive them across the country via train and ambulance (these could be horse drawn or motorised vehicles loaned for hospital transport such as a laundry van). Many of the new military hospitals opened to meet the ever-growing numbers of returned wounded during the war were established in county asylums, where the inmates had been removed to other premises such as workhouse infirmaries, and the building re-equipped especially for the reception of wounded troops.

There were also hundreds of Auxiliary War Hospitals around the country, commonly referred to as 'Red Cross Hospitals', that had been set up in private country houses, large rectories, and public buildings, funded and staffed predominantly by volunteers from the Joint War Organisation of the British Red Cross Society and Order of St John of Jerusalem

British medics and German prisoners of war help carry casualties to the Casualty Clearing Station, Somme, 1916. (Brown Family Collection)

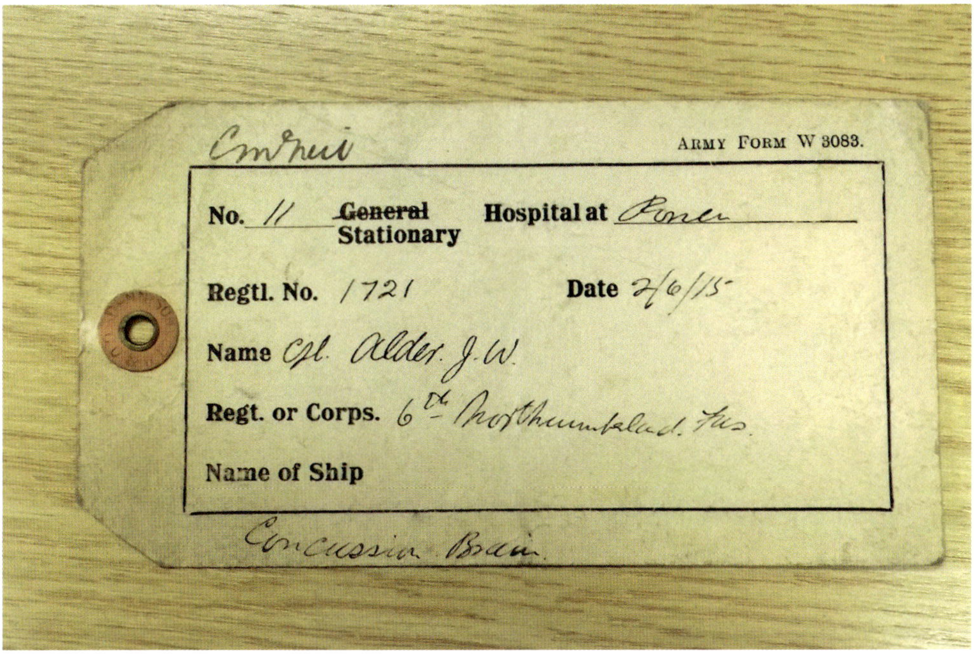

Cmdneil

ARMY FORM W 3083.

No. 11 ~~General~~ Stationary Hospital at Rouen

Regtl. No. 1721 Date 2/6/15

Name Cpl. Alder. J.W.

Regt. or Corps. 6th Northumberland. Fus.

Name of Ship

Concussion Brain

Above: This field medical tag made sure Cpl. J. W. Alder was taken to No. 11 Stationary Hospital at Rouen after he suffered concussion to his brain in June 1915.
Below: Walking wounded from the Somme waiting to board a hospital train, 1916.

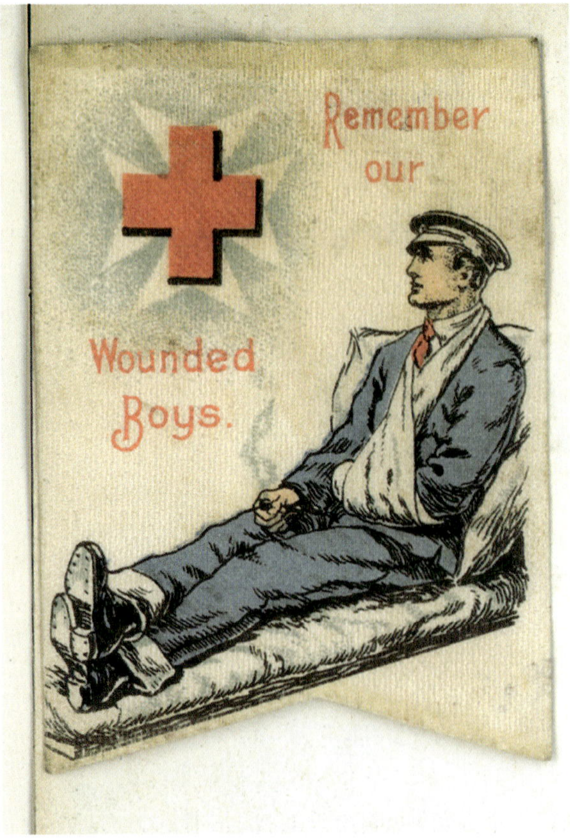

Above: Wounded but glad to be home: Red Cross nurses and convalescent soldiers at Brundall Auxiliary War Hospital *c.* 1916. (Brown Family Collection)
Left: A silk charity flag depicting a soldier in 'hospital blues' sold to raise money for local auxiliary war hospitals.

Counting the cost – a long row of graves after a big attack during the Battles of the Somme, 1916.

with a paid qualified matron and surgeon (often a local doctor). Some Auxiliary War Hospitals did provide operating theatres but in the main they were for convalescent troops. Sadly, there were still those who did not make it through and across the graveyards of Great Britain there may be found the graves of both service personnel brought back wounded from the battlefront who died in home hospitals, as well as those who died while on home service. These are all marked by the same distinctive headstones of the Commonwealth War Graves Commission that can be found all over the world.

Soldiers line up ready to board the ship that will bring them back home to 'Blighty'.

6

Goodbye to All That

The Armistice was announced at the eleventh hour of the eleventh day of the eleventh month, 1918. Public announcements were made and impromptu celebrations were held across the county but no proper celebration could be held until 'the boys came home'. With thousands of British soldiers involved in theatres of war in and far beyond the Western Front, and with the occupation forces of Germany, the campaign in north Russia, and garrison duties across the Empire still to be served, this was to be no mean feat and exactly when a man could be released from military service depended on the terms of service he had signed up for. The men who had enlisted as regular soldiers knew they would keep on serving until their years 'with the colours' had been served. However, for most of those who were volunteers or had been conscripted, they could not wait to get home again. Men with 'in demand' industrial skills, including miners, enjoyed a priority discharge, as did those who had volunteered to serve during the early war years. This left the poor old conscripts, particularly those who had turned eighteen in 1918, at the bottom of the list for 'demob'.

Once back in the UK, soldiers due for 'demob' would be sent to a Dispersal Centre. These were mostly hutted or tented temporary military camps, not necessarily anywhere near either where the soldier enlisted or his home.

At the Dispersal Centre, he would be given a Protection Certificate and a railway warrant or ticket to his chosen destination – normally the nearest station to home. This certificate also entitled the soldier to furlough (leave), pay and medical treatment if required during furlough. There was also an Out-of-Work Donation Policy book that insured him, in the event of unavoidable unemployment, for any twenty-six weeks in the year following demob. The first to be discharged were provided with a suit of plain clothes, cap, collar and tie (unless the man had procured his own in which case he was entitled to draw an allowance of 30s in respect of a suit of plain clothes.) He was also entitled to retain the cardigan waistcoat, necessaries, drawers, one pair of serviceable boots and the kitbag that had been issued to him. All other articles of uniform and clothing were to be returned to the Quartermaster before leaving the centre. But later the weight of numbers being demobbed dictated if the man chose to have a suit of plain clothes instead of an allowance (which had been raised to 52*s* 6*d*) he would be given a choice of patterns. A soldier's final leave would have begun the day after he was dispersed and he would have returned home still in uniform with his shrapnel helmet and greatcoat.

While on final furlough he was technically a soldier but fully entitled to wear plain clothes; but after twenty-eight days from dispersal he could not then wear his uniform legally. During this time, he had to hand in his greatcoat, for which he would be paid £1, which was part of his war service gratuity. His Demobilisation Ration Book could also be taken to the nearest Food Office and exchanged for an Emergency Card, which he could later exchange for a civilian Ration Book.

If not permanently disabled or serving with the Territorial Force, all soldiers were discharged into Class Z of the Army Reserve. The Class Z Reserve was authorised by Army

The mass of paperwork represents what a soldier would have had to wade though as he went through each stage of demobilisation.

Order of 3 December 1918 as a measure to enable the rapid recall of trained soldiers who had been demobbed in the event of a resumption of hostilities. The Z Reserve was abolished on 31 March 1920. Despite the complexities of demobilising an army, most of those who had served were back to Civvy Street in under a year – just in time for the National Peace Day celebrations of 19 July 1919.

Many of those who had volunteered together served together. In the staccato fire of enfilading machine guns and amid shot and shell, large numbers of men from city parishes, towns and villages fell together. The effect of such losses on these localised areas was profound. Add to the carnage on the Army the casualties of the Royal Navy and Royal Air Force serving in theatres all over the world, it is hardly surprising that by 1918 there was talk of the 'loss of a generation.' Such was the demand for mourning black that many bereaved widows had to make do with arm bands. Everyone seemed to be related to or know someone who fell and only a few lucky villages saw their menfolk leave and return unharmed from their service in 'The War to end all Wars'.

1914 - 1918

1914-15
GEORG V BRITT: OMN: REX ET IND: IMP:

Above: Paying respects to a fallen comrade on the Somme front, 1916.
Opposite above: Newcastle's war memorial, unveiled by Field Marshal Earl Haig on 23 September 1923.
Opposite below: Trio of 1914–15 Star, British War Medal and Victory Medal, otherwise known as 'Pip, Squeak and Wilfred' after cartoon characters in the *Daily Mirror*, awarded to soldiers who served through the First World War.

7
What Next?

Getting Involved

Membership of a society is not essential to learning more about the soldiers of the Great War but it can be a great way to make contacts, to find out more ways you can get involved, and to find people who share an interest in the same aspects of the First World War that you do. People who are new to the subject should not feel intimidated – we all had to start somewhere and any good historian never stops learning. I would also suggest a visit to your local studies library or to look online to see what First World War projects and exhibitions are going on in your area.

The Western Front Association
BM Box 1914, London, WC. N 3XX
http://www.westernfrontassociation.com/

The Great War Society
http://www.thegreatwarsociety.com/

Collecting

The uniforms, equipment, badges, personal effects, photographs, medals and documents of the British line infantry soldier can still be found at good quality militaria fairs today (as well as at antiques fairs, car boot sales and flea markets). Please be aware cap badges and even shoulder titles are restruck and uniforms and equipment are reproduced and can be aged and sold as originals, so I would urge caution and advise that if you are going to start buying such collectables, start at militaria fairs. Ask the fair organiser to direct you to the longest established badge or militaria dealers – there has to be a reason why they have been around for so long.

Once you purchase a few reasonably priced First World War line infantry badges (which should be around £8–£14 each) keep on with your research learning what to look for in an original item and your confidence will grow. Don't let your heart rule your head – wanting an item you fear may be a reproduction to be the real thing will not make it the real deal; neither does paying a big price for it. Never feel pressured to make a purchase. We all have passed over items we wish we had bought. Above all, take your time, learn well and enjoy collecting and researching the memorabilia of our First World War Tommies.

Here are three reliable online dealers:

The Medal Centre – http://www.themedalcentre.co.uk/
Geoff Newman Cap Badges and Insignia – http://www.gnmilitaria.co.uk/
Dear Old Blighty – http://www.dearoldblighty.com/shop.php?c=2

There are also a number of reputable dealers, militaria shops, and auction houses where quality items can be bought with confidence, such as:

DNW (Dix Noonan Webb) – https://www.dnw.co.uk/auctions/medals-and-militaria.php
Spink – https://www.spink.com/departments.aspx?id=1206

Further Reading

Brown, Malcolm – *Tommy Goes to War* (London: Butler and Tanner 1978)
Bull, Stephen – *Brassey's History of Uniforms: World War One British Army* (London: Brassey's 1998)
Chappell, Mike – *British Battle Insignia (1) 1914-18* (Botley: Osprey 1986)
Chappell, Mike – *The British Soldier of World War I* (volumes 1 and 2) (Botley: Osprey 2005)
Doyle, Peter – *Great War Tommy: Owners' Workshop Manual* (Yeovil: Haynes 2013)
Liddle, Peter H. – *The Soldiers War 1914-1918* (London: Blandford 1988)
Van Emden, Richard – *Tommy's War: The Western Front in Soldiers' Words and Photographs* (London: Bloomsbury 2014)
Westlake, Ray – *Kitchener's Army* (Tunbridge Wells: Nutshell Publishing 1989)

Places to Visit

Imperial War Museum
Lambeth Road, London, SE1 6HZ.
Established at the end of the First World War as Britain's national war museum, it's a great place to start your journey learning about the soldiers of the First World War.

Imperial War Museum (North)
The Quays, Trafford Wharf Road, Manchester M17 1TZ.
IWM (North) has powerful displays relating how war affects people's lives, has a good section of displays covering a variety of aspects of the First World War. See their website for their current temporary exhibitions. http://www.iwm.org.uk/visits/iwm-north

National Army Museum
Royal Hospital Rd, Chelsea, London SW3 4HT.
The National Army Museum is a great place to research the history of the British Army down the ages. www.nam.ac.uk

Aldershot Military Museum
Aldershot, GU11 2LG.
Tells the story of the home of the British Army from 1854 to the present day. www.hants.gov.uk/aldershot-museum

The Army Museums Ogilby Trust has a great website to help you find regimental museums relevant to your research – www.armymuseums.org.uk/amot-admin/default.asp?Category=AMOT&Service=museum-search

Web Resources

The recent upsurge in interest in the First World War had generated a huge number of new websites and forums, I would suggest starting with these five:

Imperial War Museum Collections are a superb research resource for both photographs and memorabilia relating to soldiers of the First World War. Explore the whole IWM site for events and other Great War Centenary connections.
http://www.iwm.org.uk/collections

The Long, Long Trail is a great online resource for all manner of WWI research and unit histories.
http://www.longlongtrail.co.uk/

Offers a good starting place to find out more about the Western Front Battlefields, tours, memorials, museums and archives.
http://www.greatwar.co.uk/index.htm

The National Archives offers a vast resource for anyone researching soldiers in the First World War and provides some useful online guides.
http://www.nationalarchives.gov.uk/help-with-your-research/research-guides/first-world-war/

The Commonwealth War Graves Commission is an invaluable site to help you trace fallen soldiers of the First World War. Their website also has useful information about upcoming anniversaries and commemorations.
http://www.cwgc.org/